Two Seasons

Two Seasons

Story-Poems

by

Jeanne Powell

TAUREAN HORN PRESS
Petaluma, California

Copyright 2019 © Jeanne Powell

PAPERBACK
ISBN 13: 978-0-931552-21-2

ALL RIGHTS RESERVED

These poems are copyrighted by the author and cannot be reproduced, transmitted or utilized in any form or by any means, electronic, photographic or mechanical including photocopying, recording or by any other information and storage retrieval system, without express permission in writing from the author.

Cover Photos by Kathleen Clancy
Cover Design by Mark Weiman

www.jeanne-powell.com

Manufactured in the U.S.A.
TAUREAN HORN PRESS
P.O. Box 526
Petaluma, CA 94953

ACKNOWLEDGEMENTS

Comfort Food
appeared in *World of Change* anthology, 2013

Dear Susan Delighted
appeared in *Stay Amazed* anthology,
published by Poetry Flash

Did You Know?
appeared on two websites

Dual Face of Fear and *Word Storm*
appeared in *Poets Eleven 2014* anthology
published by SF Public Library, 2014

For A Veteran
appeared on two websites

When Salome Danced
appeared in *Poets Eleven 2012 anthology*
published by SF Public Library, 2012

Every Indifferent Glance
disappeared while in the hands of
tenured professor at a major university, 2018

Table of Contents

When Autumn Came / 1
Tea Dancing / 2
"Did You Know"? / 3
Something About Mean / 4
Golden Maple Leaf / 5
Dear Susan Delighted / 6
The Gifts I Bring / 7
Long Memories / 8
Dining Out / 9
Jesus is Back / 10
Deserve More / 11
Tatiana in Winter / 12
Dual Face of Fear / 13
Comfort Food / 14
When Salome Danced / 15
For a Veteran / 16
Chronicles of Marin / 18
Do Not Hang Up / 19
The Noise of Tomorrow / 20
Every Indifferent Glance / 21
Kicking Up A Sound / 22
A Writing Prayer / 23
And Then He Went To Whiskey / 24
So He Moved To Boston / 26

Word Storm / 27
Darkness Has A Cutting Edge / 29
Getting Out of the Swamp / 30
A Path to the Door / 31
Sarah Fades From View / 32
Baby Panda With Sunflowers / 33
What Shall I Listen To? / 34
You Never Brought Me Flowers / 35
Letter to a Sibling Gone / 36
Without A Sound / 37
Her Red Blouse / 38
Don't Talk About the Flowers / 39
He Looked A Lot Like Money / 40
Why I Don't Ask Questions / 41
Cassie On The Rocks / 42
About Those Missing Plums / 43
A Mountain In Ireland / 44
She Kept Calling Time / 45
Nanking Where I Fell In Love / 46
Westward Ho / 47
The Hardest Job / 48
She Doesn't Get Involved / 49
Emergency / 50
Safe Surrender Site / 51
Thoughts Upon Awakening / 52

Story-Poems

When Autumn Came

Restive talk in the air
rumors apace
before autumn slid under the gates
spilled over retaining walls
flew in doors left ajar

a short and brutal spring
impatient to get out of town
startled by cries for help
and storms out of season

summer came crashing
with a lot of baggage
settled in for the long haul
memorable in its blasts
and heated exchanges
with sudden squalls

when autumn sauntered
through town one sultry night
intimations of mortality cooled passions
and gratitude awakened
from a troubled sleep

hints of frost tarried
along manicured hedges
a long slow slide anticipated
into numbing chill
but for now, for now
autumn was here.

© 2019 Jeanne Powell

Tea Dancing

She likes it with a little cream
this tawny tea from Cedarberg
green hills in the south of Africa
she heard they harvested in summer
let the herb ferment a while
then dried it in the streaming sun
deep red, deep red mahogany

she likes her wordsongs deeply brewed
so they linger nightlong round and open
in sweet cellars of the soul
then burst out feather bright
to word-dance with the morning light
consuming doubts and random fears
divinely sprawled on luscious leaves

she likes it with a little cream
this bingo bango mango black
tea bold pot of turbulence
dripping rich ripe leafy chant
ocean pearls in her curly hair
every steaming cup she drinks
emancipated sparkling glow

she likes it with a little cream.

"Did You Know"?

[Fruitvale BART station,
Oakland CA, January 1, 2009]

*my country 'tis of thee
sweet land of liberty
of thee I sing*

did you know before today
a bullet fired in disdain,
callous indifference
into a young father's back
as he lies face down on harsh cement
will power through, race through
his body prone
bounce off the pavement cold
and splash back into vital organs
like the heart and spirit and soul,
leaving no room for compromise,
explanation or forgiveness
and no time to say goodbye
to his lovely baby daughter?

but you know now…

of thee I sing

[for Oscar Grant]

© 2019 Jeanne Powell

Something About Mean

heard a lot about guns lately
a few machetes and knives across the pond
but mostly guns.
my ex telephoned last week
first time in 20 years
wanted to know when
we could get together
for the sake of old times.
he's a millionaire on paper now, he offered.
sooo I said maybe … and
we met at the ferry building
just as the fishing boats were coming in.
we ate fish and chips under early morning fog.

what I remember most about him
was the way he handled guns.
all his life he handled guns,
big ones, shotguns, rifles,
never saw the need for handguns.
in all his life
he never had an accident.
never drank while shooting,
never missed a target,
never fired in anger.
never pointed a gun at a human;
where he came from
that was just plain mean.

and he knew something about mean.

Golden Maple Leaf

Forever
recall this
golden maple leaf
dancing
gleefully inside
autumn breezes, minutes
before
winter intervenes
demanding a beguine
bolero
castle walk
flamenco, galliard, gavotte
habanera
hornpipe, lindy
mazurka, meringue, minuet
salsa
samba, shimmy
snake dance, tango
celebrating
nutmeg memories
before hibernation reigns.

Dear Susan Delighted
[happy birthday!]

We talked in Glen Park
the subject was birthdays
continually of interest
individual destinies
dictated by the stars
before conception
on any earthly level.

Were we here at first
this galaxy, or another?
cannot fathom the concept
of another universe or two
and so limit myself
to the titillation
of galaxy hopping
in this universe
one millennium to the next

Andromeda, Omega, Virgo,
Centaurus, the Milky Way,
Pleiades cluster especially.
sailing beyond the direction of sunset
until we transform and live again
among our sibling stars, seed stars,
every midnight a new birth
under Orion's strong shield.

© 2019 Jeanne Powell

The Gifts I Bring

tequila for your empty nights
zinfandel from Trader Joe's
funny stories to make you smile
poems in books and from the heart
the healing joy of laughter

prayers for all your loved ones
spiritual books to keep you safe
films old and new to help you escape
forgiveness in word and deed
acceptance of who you are

please enjoy these gifts I bring
feel worthy of acceptance
be free of judgment and complaint
so that I may return next week
and bring you even more.

© 2019 Jeanne Powell

Long Memories
[for the elephants]

A man reflects upon elephants.
He loves them and lives for them,
sees the terrible danger
as they push to defend
their traditional grazing lands
from humans who tamper with natural order
and procreate into multitudes,
spilling into elephant walks and trails,
laying claim and laying siege.
He must save them, but how?
In his desperation this man
becomes brilliant and brave
and blazes new trails
in species preservation.
He trains domesticated elephants
to fight their wild brethren,
patrol the shifting boundaries
and challenge their wild cousins
with chilling trumpets and tusks flaring.
The wild ones are at a disadvantage,
not knowing the game or its high stakes
and finally give way before
this bizarre aggression
led by a man on the back of an elephant.
The wild ones retreat
to live another season
or perhaps to go mad
from the unreality of shrinking ground,
and so cannot return to thank the man
who loves elephants so much
that he organized an army of them
to keep their wild brethren
out of the range of farmers' guns
for one more season.

© 2019 Jeanne Powell

Dining Out

we sat outside the Mission Street café
cradled in mismatched rocking chairs
full of trips down memory lane.
do you have any discounts? we asked
not in this lifetime, the owner grinned.

plunging in, we ordered southern chicken,
potatoes mashed and gravied,
a vinegar touch on the collard greens,
sweet dates wrapped in thick bacon strips,
followed by bourbon pecan pie
and a little vanilla ice cream.

the owner liked our style.
he sent over tiny cornbread muffins
and a side of steamed asparagus,
compliments of the house.

we spoke of other women's lovers
who still lived in the 'hood
and ranked them according to
the heartache they had caused.

we rated our various brilliant careers
in states too numerous to mention,
and agreed that not working at all
rivaled anything we had done.

and we drank to that, more than once.

© 2019 Jeanne Powell

Jesus Is Back

Jesus is back
He has returned
I wanted to give you the news
in case you missed Nightline
on ABC News last June.

He is living on a farm
in the Russian mountains, due east
when He's ready, He will descend,
but I'm thinking
it will not be soon.

ABC News sent a journalist
by plane and truck and train
when they heard about His return.
the journalist waited three days
at the farm while Jesus meditated,
then came out to greet her.

They sat on bales of hay
surrounded by mountains
and His long hair flowed
as He answered her queries,
small though they were.

When He knew she saw Him
only as a new age rock star
He arose and said farewell.

Even God is unhappy with ABC News
now that Ted Koppel
and Peter Jennings
have gone.

Ted Koppel anchored ABC Nightline for years before retiring.
Peter Jennings anchored ABC Evening News until he died.

© 2019 Jeanne Powell

Deserve More
[Hurricane Katrina – New Orleans – 2005]

A properly raised man
does not evacuate
does not eliminate
will never defecate
in a public place
there are women and children
you understand?
basic proprieties
outweigh mere survival
after all
life's daily indignities
require so much
energy to overcome
racism
bigotry
hot weather meanness
so you sit
with dignity sandbagged
day after day
in the amphitheater from hell
and take Kaopectate
until you die.

Tatiana In Winter
(San Francisco zoo in 2007)

Tiger glowing, tiger bright
in the dust of urban blight
I know that She who made the lamb
gave birth to thee

beauty mysterious
caged and philosophical
till someone called you out to play
never envisioning
you would up-end their mad foray

manners razor sharp and focused
you dispatched unwary hosts
never dreaming
your seeming lack of "affect"
would condemn you

tiger glowing, tiger bright
in the dust of urban blight
Siberian
so far from home
we miss you.

© 2019 Jeanne Powell

Dual Face of Fear

In my city
walking along my streets
looking like the visitor you are
you give me that look that says
you are questioning my credentials
my authenticity
my right to be here
in my city

Walking in my direction
you suddenly notice
my golden brown roundness
and show all those attitudes
entertain all those postures
grabbing your purse
and holding it close in
as I walk past you

Let me tell you something
all the while you brush past me
wearing African jewelry and corn-row braids
a touch of blackness in fashion where you come from
while you clutch your designer knockoff
making me unwelcome in my own 'hood
when I walk by, on my sidewalk
let me tell you something

You clearly cannot tell the difference
between what is real and what is fake --
so listen up real good, wench
if I wanted to, I could remove
your fake face and paste it
on that designer knockoff
but since no part of you is real
why should I bother?

© 2019 Jeanne Powell

Comfort Food
[for the people of Haiti]

under a burning sun
Marie crouched in the marketplace all day
watchful and lean
her 5 cent pies were the best in the business
and business was brisk.
early in the week Marie worried
the wagon from the mountains was late
she needed the special dirt
trucked into Port au Prince twice a week

and the weather caused her to frown
overcast skies were bad for business
she needed the sun to be harsh and unrelenting
like the politicians and soldiers
so she could bake.
but first the mixing
rich mountain dirt, then precious water,
sugar from broken cane stalks,
herbs rescued from dry earth
and stir and stir
then shape the pies by hand

lay them out, like corpses
lining the boulevard when there is war
and there is never-ending war
lay out the mud pies to dry
crucial to have a harsh and fiery sun
her thin body bent over the pies
bent down in gratitude to the sun

the good weather held all week
fresh mud pies were ready to sell
her people were starving so business was good
and in the soft breezes at midnight
the ghost of Toussaint L'Ouverture
wailed through streets stained with blood.

When Salome Danced

Vigilant in the warm dark
they sat shoulder to shoulder
glad to be together again
the passion of Salome
igniting center stage.
He careful to stay in his allotted space
she curious about the change in him
share the arm rest she said
no I'm too warm he whispered
as though his body heat were
any more distracting than hers.
Nesting deep in orchestra seats
his strength and her passion in supernova
as Salome sang out in trance, ensnared and danced
Strauss, enchanted by Oscar's wild story,
lacking restraint or remorse onstage.
But lifeless lips were not her passion
his heated words in that darkness
would not require his life's blood
to splash across her golden breasts.
Rest, she said, her silver locks
brushing his tawny curls
you are safe here – for now
you are safe here.
Rest.

© 2019 Jeanne Powell

For a Veteran

Weekend like any other, running in a light rain, catch a bus
and then a train. Destination? Bookseller in Glen Park --
publication party in progress and my friend Bill was
featured. Reading finished, we wanted to drink a toast
to poetry at a café nearby, but Bill kept pausing to listen
to a thin man with silver hair and intensity, his voice
baked in years of combat long ago and far away,
yet still this day and every day.

Half listening to their talk and impatient to be going,
I pointed to my wrist watch in mute appeal and
pulled Bill out the door and down the hill.
Elated by the reading, we perched on café chairs,
talked of spoken word adventures and in time recalled
the man who found a kindred spirit in my pacifist friend
and poured out words unrehearsed and never written.

I asked Bill why the man kept speaking in long sentences
held close, as though imparting a secret. Bill said the man who
barely spoke above a whisper was Marcus, and he served in our
many undeclared wars. He would be serving still but for the
heart attack in Iraq, stressed from worrying about the 19 year olds
who did not know enough to fear death. He wanted to stand
in the dusty fields and catch them before they stumbled into
harm's way. Marcus could not save them all. His heart
exploded from the effort, so the government sent him home.

Now he felt well enough most days, well enough to walk and tell
his story to anyone who would listen, and I felt saddened by his
loss, his many losses, in our undeclared wars. To save yourself, he
said had to tear down the wall of ice which kept forming around
you, do anything to tear it down. Marcus worked on farms
in the Imperial Valley, shirt stripped off in summer heat,
worked until his back burned red and fiery pain

© 2019 Jeanne Powell

melted the wall of ice enough so he could stay alive.
He said you had to know how to tear holes in that wall
if you wanted to survive, back here, back in the world.

A bristling noonday sun presents differently now, summons
images of fire and ice for Bill, and I wish we knew how to
say that to Marcus, how to say that to all the others whose
hearts we broke on our way to unforgiving empire.

© 2019 Jeanne Powell

Chronicles of Marin

Dishwater Blonde with husband sick in Mill Valley,
she aimed right for your sunny San Rafael bedroom,
and you never even saw her coming.
She looked to you for comfort and inspiration
all the while it was your husband she wanted to inspire.
But you, silly 'burbanite, trained your misguided telescope
on the sparkling brown Dancer from the big city,
where you heard all real sin originated.

Well, it all came down to the Petaluma Poetry Walk
that third absurd Sunday, in weather hot and wet.
Some kind of fool you were to stay in San Rafael
while Dishwater Blonde got on the poetry bus,
exposing all her intentions in tight white leather.
Awash in blue eye shadow, she gave your husband
a world tour, a trick that put your myopia to shame,
rolling that poetry bus all over the freeway.

Foolishly you stayed home, dust growing on your telescope
trusting Dishwater Blonde because she was, well, blonde.
Dancer from the big city had to stop being your friend.
CityGirl knew a missed conception when she saw one.
Dancer had to drop you in the middle of that blue eyeshadow
and hope you overcame cluelessness before tight white leather
put you in the same grave as her ailing husband.

Just saying, you should have seen it coming --
your husband's wandering eye, her habitual hangdog hunger,
that ailing husband routine she dropped on your coffee table.
Next time, the very next time, put on your high-heeled sneakers
and GET ON THE BUS, GET ON THE BUS,
GET ON THE BUS.

© 2019 Jeanne Powell

Do Not Hang Up

Do not hang up. This could be the most important call of your life. Our records show you to be crafty and concealing in your thinking, even though you have received 22 Notices of Opportunity to open your mind to the state in the interest of national security.

From sun reflector morning to mandatory nightshade and beyond, the national security office struggles to provide you with the safety essential to our post-apocalyptic society. Simply share your thoughts with us continually, so the V.I.R.U.S. project may cleanse them of contagious impurities.

You have served the community so well, working in the Soylent Green factory and participating in the cleaning of our electronic guillotines. Each potential renegade [PR] is allowed 25 Notices of Opportunity before public execution is offered as an option one cannot refuse.

Upon sober and serious reflection,
every moment of which should be shared with us,
we know you will not fail to reach a patriotic decision.

Virtual Inquiry Replacement Under Surveillance
The V.I.R.U.S. Project

© 2019 Jeanne Powell

The Noise of Tomorrow

LOOK, I don't know how I got here.
Some celestial contract in the Akashic Records,
or a spacecraft ran out of fuel, whatever.
There may have been some colossal misunderstanding
back in the day, an angst-ridden war among the gods.
One minute we are progressing on a picture-perfect
planet and the next millennium or two we are
at each other's throats in constant mesmerizing warfare.
I'M TELLING YOU, I honestly don't know how I got here.
And about those five-year plans and ten-year plans – do you
seriously believe I ever thought about either option?
I'm here by accident, remember? There was no grand design,
at least none that I am willing to recall.
Did my planet disintegrate, like Krypton,
or my magical island disappear into the mists when
faith took a holiday?
I'm the Lady of the Lake without my Avalon or
the last temple priestess after the collapse of Atlantis.
How on earth do you expect me to plan for tomorrow?
IT'S TOO NOISY HERE! Too many people with no room for
dignified retreats where you wander alone on an icy windswept
shore. Babies are crying for lost mothers, mothers are crying for
disappeared children, women are widowed for profit,
and the old are without wisdom.
LOOK, I did not bargain for all this. As a matter of fact, I may not
have been allowed to bargain at all – some bearded guy holding
tablets written in stone, an oracle or two from a cave in Greece.
Will I ever get a recount of any votes? An appeal to a higher court?
The noise of tomorrow is here today, and
I need ear plugs, and a game plan, and a witness.
CAN I GET A WITNESS?

© 2019 Jeanne Powell

Every Indifferent Glance

Very clear he was
about his outcome in life
work with what you know
work with what you have
first person care is the rule.
let every glance be indifferent
to others, once you are clear
they pose no threat.

She was small in that corner of the alley.
he typed her, then ignored her
with every indifferent glance.
Stretching under a thin red coat
shivering, every breath she took
so small in that corner of the alley
not worthy of a serious look
in his backgammon world.

Rose where did you?
sprinted through his memory
quickstepping past old pain
Rose where did you get?
that other one had been a mini
in her merry-girl crimson shawl
all those many months ago.
Rose where did you get that red?

No one remembered her story
too many other tales of distress.
Now he shrugged and repositioned
his hard-won nonchalance
all through evening shadows
so that every indifferent glance
could find this new one more quickly
in case she lasted through the night.

© 2019 Jeanne Powell

Kicking Up A Sound

without kicking up a sound
the lone-wolf brunette
wipes her tears with a cigarette
leans on a cast iron bench

she makes her face a mask
except for olive flares in her eyes
waiting in patient shadow
beneath a blanket of winter

still too far from heaven
she remembers dandelion thistles
knows winter can be forgiving
to the last hardy peach of summer.

A Writing Prayer

I write the way I pray
sporadically
and with the mind of a skeptic.
I know She is there, in there,
out here in the golden flowers
drooping between tree branches,
in shadows dancing on air currents.
Her eye is on the sparrow
and I fear She sees me too well
this Muse, forgiving Mother of us all,
and yet Taskmaster stirring the pot,
admonishing us to measure up,
toughen up, to our greatness
inherent at birth.
For we poets are the chosen ones
and everything depends on that sunbeam
gracing the flight pattern of a honey bee,
and the cloud cover aiding the journey
of a snow leopard.
For we poets are the chosen ones
as surely as a red-tailed hawk dives
from a mountain
to a forest of feasting.

© 2019 Jeanne Powell

And Then He Went To Whiskey

She: I don't want to leave you, not really.

He: Why did you even come into my life?

She: You know we can't live together any more.

He: Why didn't you say something in Portland?

She: I wasn't with you in Portland. You only imagined I was there.

He: You smoke too damned much and drink too much wine.

She: If you didn't kill a bottle of whiskey every night, you would remember things.

He: You wear purple pjs to bed instead of those negligees I bought you. How come?

She: The other week you called me Margaret, and before that, you called me Hillary.

He: Is it my fault you change your name all the time?

She: I was Margaret on Grey's Anatomy, and I was Hillary on Saturday Night Live.

He: You're never home anyway. Always going to Portland.

She: I've never been in Portland. I go to Seattle when you are away.

© 2019 Jeanne Powell

He: My phone says you're calling from Portland. I know how to read.

She: You don't read area codes accurately. And you can't read me at all.

He: Forget area codes. You are a closed book with empty pages.

She: Then why do you wish to have me stay?

He: Those negligees were custom made, and won't fit anyone else. Damned expensive too.

She: Elliott doesn't want me to sleep in anything.

He: I can have him killed, you know. I have friends in Portland.

She: Elliott happens to be in Seattle, where I am going now.

He: If I could move, I would kill you.

She: That has been your fantasy for some time now. Settle differences by threatening to kill.

He: I'm too drunk to kill you now, but the thought will stay with me.

She: If you ever get sober again, you won't remember, and you'll look for me in Portland.
 [she leaves the room]

He: [sipping whiskey] Don't you want to finish your pinot noir? It was a good year, and expensive.

So He Moved To Boston

Portland wasn't working. She seemed to be everywhere,
although he knew this was not so, because his spies
said she was still in Seattle. What is she doing there,
he fumed, hanging out at the fish market and collecting
more hashish pipes?

He vowed to stay in Portland for a while because the city
received good reviews in Sunday supplements and
the restaurants were trendy. He liked "trendy" because
when he dined in such a place he felt as though he were
in the moment and his life were happening now instead of
being buried in the past, in a basement next to an
abandoned well and a ramshackle barn on the far side
of a marsh, adjacent to a dead-end road.
But Portland wasn't working anymore.

So he moved to Boston, instructing his spies to stay on the job
in Seattle. He moved to Boston with its bloodsucking heat
and merciless snow, its crabby buildings and overcrowded
history, its clam chowder attitude and welcome proximity
to the ocean. For the ocean bathed you in icy forgiveness,
 welcomed you without reservation, as no one else could.

© 2019 Jeanne Powell

Word Storm

Saturday night adventure in the blinding rain.
GK telephones from Vallejo. Come watch him feature
and share my new poem with him during open mic.
But it's Vallejo, so what can I do? Cable car, ferry boat,
then a long walk. Am I up for this?

Once I asked GK if he liked living in that cozy town
with his new love, whether it was a good place to move.
No f*cking way. I mean, no f*cking way. There is
no f*cking way you should ever move to f*cking Vallejo,
f*cking ever, do you f*cking hear me? He made his point.

The magic day arrived but it was pouring rain, pouring felines
and canines with dolphins thrown in. The raindrops had gills.
I gathered my good luck charms in a spiritual huddle and off
we went in a wet and windy downpour. Anything for poetry,
I said, anything at all.

My London Fog umbrella suffered near fatal damage
in the last rainstorm, caught in a vitriolic burst of hail outside
the Sears Roebuck building on Masonic. But it still had a few
 minutes of service remaining, so I propped it open and
ventured into the storm.

I forged a path through the rain, from cable car to ferry boat
in record time. That little ferry rocked and rolled all the way
to Vallejo, while I downed red wine to keep my courage dry.
My cantankerous friend was celebrating a birthday in a town
he hated, but in a café he loved, and I promised to be there.

Suddenly there I was onstage at the café, during open mic
with a passel of musicians, while it rained outside like there
was no tomorrow. I recited my new poem about love in a
menstrual storm, genuinely tipsy in a whiskey-fueled glow,
 feeling wonderfully grand on a rain-soaked Saturday night.
And GK, well, he roared with delight.

© 2019 Jeanne Powell

So there we were – rough cider, menstrual joys,
poetry in the raw, footstomping jazz, pesky
raindrops whistling round the roof, red wine
flowing, and my birthday poet friend laughing
as though he were back in Manhattan
and free of California detours forever.

Darkness Has A Cutting Edge

Darkness has a cutting edge
kept sharp and ready
deep in shadow, waiting
for those who fail to trust
the rightness of dark
who misuse it to hide their deeds.

Darkness has a mission
a purpose, is an invitation to
rich ripe deep thinking
recreating the universe
in slices of brilliance.

Darkness is an invitation
to dare, dream, dynamite
decrepit distractions keeping
you from sunlight.

Darkness is a keen friend
to its sunny cousin, descends
when requested and gives
yearly deferrals to lands of the
Midnight Sun.

I stay on the good side
of darkness.
I always want to know
the difference
between day and night.

© 2019 Jeanne Powell

Getting Out of the Swamp

That swamp
you know
where you sit
most of the time
other names
rainforest, everglades
but you know
its real name
where you stop
writing, creating
where you stop
going for the basket
where you stop
dreaming about tomorrow
where you stop breathing
until your chest heaves
gasping, clutching air
yeah
searching for
that basketball hoop?
get off the bench
get out of yesterday
get writing, creating
dribble down the court
do it now
remember,
the alligators are waiting.

© 2019 Jeanne Powell

A Path to the Door

Edward knew he could not leave this woman, ever.

Ellis was older than he, but she could beat him at
table tennis and croquet.

She slept late into the morning, but would stay up
all night to nurse him through a sinus attack or
just plain night terrors.

Ellis hated his wallpaper sister and his moonfaced
brother-in-law, but never failed to prepare the
best roasted quail when they came to dinner.
It was their favorite.

When Edward crashed and burned as he failed
in one business venture after another, Ellis sighed
then took another bite out of their trust fund
so their way of life would not be interrupted.

Of course, he was never sure it was their trust fund
since she did not share the paperwork, but Ellis
assured him that all was well.

Even when Ellis flew into quiet rages over misplaced bets
on race horses and sports teams, ripping apart his clothing
rather than hers, Edward stayed put.

With that woman's wit and rage,
girth and culinary greatness,
there never seemed to be a clear path to the door.

© 2019 Jeanne Powell

Sarah Fades From View

Simply stated, she is exquisite, sitting in her circle of tranquility.
After all, at 95 years of age, she has seen a lot. She recalls
long lazy summer days on an Oregon farm, growing up
with three brothers, including one who brought her sadness.
And she recalls much about 70 years of marriage to a wry
and witty doctor, a union yielding two children, boy and girl.

Dr. William left her early this year offering terse farewells
before calling his son and telling him "it's time." Wed to an
oxygen tent, Dr. William read and re-read James Joyce and
Leo Tolstoy in an armchair next to a sun-bright window,
waiting for the day, waiting for the moment, at age 102.

Accustomed to being taken for granted, Sarah had toiled gently
in a sun-filled home in the middle of a city, raising children,
playing the piano, and learning to play the flute,
drawing comfort from poetry and wildflowers. Reading
sheet music was just one of her accomplishments.

These days her children live far away, and Sarah speaks mostly
to her brown-skinned nurses from Manila and Katmandu, who
attend her 24 hours. But Sarah misses William, and is annoyed
that Mina and Amelie hide her walker to keep her from falling.

A Fred Astaire movie on tv or Olympic ice skating stars may
pique her interest, take her back to silver-edged moments.
When read aloud, the poetry of Stevie Smith elicits laughter.
Blueberry tea and homemade pear cake lighten her spirits
on sunny afternoons.

Slowly, though, ever so slowly, Sarah is fading from view.
The past calls too loudly, our voices here grow too soft.
We gather each day and surround her with love,
but a stronger pull prevails. Our lovely Sarah smiles into
yesterday, the sun pales, as she slowly fades from view.

© 2019 Jeanne Powell

Baby Panda With Sunflowers

Life in a third floor walk-up with a widow who is a harridan was not exciting. Baby Panda yearned for more sunlight and better conversation, a little laughter now and then. Her black and white faux fur perked up at the sound of merriment coming from the apartment below when the widow opened a window. Didn't Dashiell Hammett used to live there?

Panda was sure small talk would be more intriguing downstairs, instead of listening to the widow complain about the price of loose tea and the cost of having her toenails painted blue every two weeks. She just knew that the widow's late husband would wish more and a better fate for Baby Panda.

The big break came Thursday morning when Panda turned a deaf ear to the widow's loud whine and clanging of copper pots. One cold shoulder led to another and before she knew it, Baby Panda had been taken downstairs and tossed into a blue bin at the curb.

Well, this new development is promising, Baby Panda thought and waited for the next turn. She heard footsteps and suddenly saw sunlight. A Good Samaritan had opened the blue bin. Gently rescuing Panda and a bouquet of sunflowers, the stranger placed both on top of the bin and then walked away, adjusting his giant headphones as he did so.

Now we're getting somewhere, Baby Panda said to herself as she glanced around Post Street and patted the still lively sunflowers. Happy to meet you, she said to her flowery friends. We can travel together if you like,
and they nestled comfortably atop
the blue bin as they awaited the approach of new friends.

© 2019 Jeanne Powell

What Shall I Listen To?

This blissful emptiness, this quietly gray basket of waiting
I have been hearing, hearing the voices of memory
lightning swift whispers squeezed from low flying clouds
then from raindrops full of tumbling musical letters

    >>we love you now and always<<
    >>don't leave us behind<<
    >>we'll give you a task<<
    >>to edge merriment and mischief<<
    >>closer to your life<<

I listen and shiver:

what shall I steal today?
an overripe mango from my kitchen,
a paperback writer ready to bloom,
copper skillets lolling on sidewalks,
wildest of strawberries from empty fields,
my old self back from the wars?

what shall I listen to?
scraping of bowls in grandmother's kitchen,
yesterday's laughter again and again,
the sweetness from when it was so much sweeter,
a drumstick greeting a plastic bucket,
a mariner whistling up bold sea tales,
hardy hydrangeas near a courtyard bench?

If I melt down the wax in all of my ears
and close all my eyes with softness
those merry voices will return
be more than just a memory
will dance again from street to street
and walk through walls with me forever.

© 2019 Jeanne Powell

You Never Brought Me Flowers

Remember that day at the races when my horse won
against all odds, and I bet on him because he reminded
me of my grandfather's thoroughbred in the Great War?
You never brought me flowers and I felt like a champion
that day as the crowd roared, and I expected – yes I
realize now I expected – a bouquet of yellow roses.

There is a man who talks to me when I walk
in MacArthur Park near the swans. He brings me flowers.
We speak of many subjects and he never fails to offer
daisies, or tulips or dahlias as the season dictates.

That time I said I was going to visit Cousin Lydia because
she felt blue after the death of her fourth husband?
I lied. She took me to a doctor across the border and he
fixed things so I never have to bear another child
of yours.

And that third child I gave birth to? You never brought me
flowers then either. The third child you love so much? His
biological father actually is the milkman, you know, the butter
and egg man, a man who understands sweet spots and
magic moments.

Keep the house. I'm taking the cottage in the south of France.
If you fight me, I'll find a way to reclaim that condo you bought
for your teenage mistress in Brooklyn? Brooklyn! Really?
You should have done better.

© 2019 Jeanne Powell

Letter to a Sibling Gone

Do they have windows where you are now?
Is it even necessary to place panes of glass between
your new normalcy and the rest of this world?
If you have those panes reflecting light and
shadows, what are they made of?
Do your windows dissolve and reform like those
worm holes in science fiction space?

Without windows you would have no need for
drapes or curtains, shades or blinds, shutters or awnings.
Without windows here on earth, think of all the
people who would be without employment, the ones
who create or adorn our repetition of windows --
who replace them when they break, who enhance
their undeniable beauty with different frames and
shards of multicolored glass.

Some days I see your memory reflected in bright
glistening of mobiles and freshly washed coins,
and sometimes you lurk ever so gently
in the panes of unconscious thoughts.
Perhaps I'll never know why you went to a better place,
but I thank you so much for remembering to visit
in the many windows of my soul.

© 2019 Jeanne Powell

Without A Sound

A front door closes without a sound. A woman is leaving
her family and does not want to wake the children. Her
husband died a month ago and now is the time for her
to bolt for freedom, while she still has a chance.

She is not heartless. After all, she is taking the toddler
with her. The other three are old enough to live in real time.
She had to run away from home when she was 16. And
she has to run away now.

She had put in her time for so many years --
in factories and restaurants, cooking and cleaning,
giving birth to four children, enduring
loneliness and isolation because neighbors in the
Great Lakes did not like her east coast ways.

Her time was now. Moving quietly, the way she does,
she filled the house with chicken roasting and biscuits
baking. Her silences grew deeper. She dreamed of a life
on the west coast, where you could hear the ocean roar.

The children were sleeping now, deep in their dreams.
Yet even in their sleeping moments the young ones could feel
her leaving them, long before the morning sunlight,
long before the front door opened and closed.

© 2019 Jeanne Powell

Her Red Blouse

a Saturday anything but rain-splashed
squeeze and breeze sits tableside
ready to splash cooling water
should my writing match the angry
scarlet shade of that red blouse and
cause the poet to be scarred.

a morning of promise as I reach
for a new experience in my cedar closet
anything light-hearted hanging between
black silk mystery and green hemp playful.
instead, I discover this blouse dripping
wine red smoldering, from where?

I recall two Januarys ago, just off
the world's edge, my only sister's funeral
the obligatory closet crawl afterward
with solicitous nieces eager to strip their shelves
of memory. Here, Auntie, take this,
take this home and wear it.

things I have carried in this life
her meanness early on, her timeless glamour,
and now this red blouse, seashell buttons
hidden from all who failed to bear witness
to her many harsh absences.

to fasten each intricate seashell button
another aggravation from the past
then slip the blouse over one's neck
the magic begins with the slip-up and over
sister, sister, where are you now?

© 2019 Jeanne Powell

Don't Talk About the Flowers

begonias, tiffany roses,
black-eyed susans
snapdragons,
I gave everything I had.

these last minute tributes
and phony funerals
gathering people,
I mean, who really cares?

snatching up flowers
holding back whiskey
until the preacher finishes.
did anyone notice when he was alive?

No!
so why all the fuss now?
And don't talk about the flowers.
I gave everything I had.

© 2019 Jeanne Powell

He Looked A Lot Like Money

Our history professor maintained an air of warmth
shared fleetingly as he hurried toward a better tomorrow.
Always ready to answer questions after a lecture,
he bustled around the lectern collecting his notes,
flashing a megawatt smile beneath probing eyes.

One day he focused on cousin Lydia, making a point
of noticing her in the audience as he delivered his talk
on the excesses of the French Revolution. Sensitive
to admiring glances, cousin Lydia took to wearing
emerald necklaces and silver earrings becomingly.

After class a few weeks later, the professor invited her
to dinner at a fashionable steakhouse in a popular
neighborhood. He wore a golden-hued necktie and a
fragrance which hinted at hairpin turns and other hazards.

Still, cousin Lydia suspected nothing of his inclinations
until she made an indiscreet remark over profiteroles and
cappuccino. I'm living carefully now since the market crash,
she confided. The warmth in his hazel eyes died as suddenly
as a lit match goes out in a snowstorm.

Blinded by candlelight and his honeyed tones of voice,
Cousin Lydia had not realized his true worth.
but then gigolos have to make a living too, she decided.
after all was said and done, she liked to say to friends,
he looked a lot like money.

© 2019 Jeanne Powell

Why I Don't Ask Questions

was it last year, no Tuesday before last,
you said, why don't I ask you things?
I stammered a while, the way I do
when you ask me stuff.
I took your question under advisement.
I mean, since time ignores me anyway,
I might as well let go thinking about it,
but I do recall your question.
See, asking you requires me, no, demands…
see, I can't even phrase it right.
Pulling words out of that tangle of
phrases called language
and answering to "demands" and
"requirements", so far above my pay grade.
Don't even bother to figure out
the how and why of that statement.
So, asking you means getting clear on the question
I may wish to ask, then needing to create
a response to your answer and all that,
so you see why I don't ask.
But I do owe you a response…did I just give you one?
Oh, that's a question. Forgive me.

© 2019 Jeanne Powell

Cassie On The Rocks

She walks as though she knows
where she is going and how to get there.
She talks as though the listener understands.
She is Cassandra.
But this time, they really should listen.

She laughs and they feel empowered beyond reason.
She walks through doors as though anyone can,
doors sealed shut with the blood and bones
of martyrs with livers torn and trashed.
Random words surface, but no one hears.

When she dances, weapons to the ready,
flashing emeralds and rubies to disguise defenses,
they see only the sweet slow grace of her movements.
She shelters the wounded
with reassuring conversation or a smile,
a blessing sent across a crowded train,
and they are pleased without knowing why.

At home after midnight, shedding armor
and arrows and magical wrist bands,
she examines wounds that never heal,
memories that never fade, and realizes
not for the first time
she has made it all seem too easy.

© 2019 Jeanne Powell

About Those Missing Plums

William Carlos! Where are you?
every time I need something
you seem to be absent
doctoring someone else

What on earth?
William, what is this note
on the icebox
about my fresh plums?

What have you done?
where are my cold plums?
Martin brought them for me.
I wanted those plums!

Do you have to leave your mark
on everybody and everything?
your papers on my sewing table?
your apple peels on my couch?

You are not a plum catch anymore
you need to think about me.
I can be sweet and delicious
with someone else!

© 2019 Jeanne Powell

A Mountain In Ireland

She named her daughter after a mountain in Ireland. I was struck by this remark, which Sisi volunteered over afternoon coffee at La Boulangerie. We spoke of a mutual friend whose marriage had fallen on hard times. In keeping with the sparkling sunshine and a white parrot on someone's shoulder nearby, Sisi and I quickly moved to happier times in our friend's marriage when she traveled all over Europe and the UK, secure in her husband's love and devotion.

Her daughter was conceived in Ireland after a long walk through legendary monuments. Our mutual friend loved Ireland for its ancient forests and heroic warriors and its fiercely aloof mountains. I marveled at how often we think we know all about a person but actually know only that person's contemporary surface, glimpsed over baked salmon and artichokes served with a unremarkable chardonnay.

Sisi and I drank a second cup of strong coffee, then switched to another topic of conversation – daffodils. Easy to do when someone walks by with a stately Saint Bernard on a long leash and a wicker basket of daffodils. How very fresh those yellow flowers looked, even though their natural life had been snapped when garden shears cut through the stems.

Very much like people in some ways, Sisi murmured. How so, I asked? Well, we sometimes shine brightest when we are cut off from our "natural" lives – the ones we plan – and are keeping up a brave front until we can assess the damage and cover up the wound. No time to heal yet – just stem the bleeding and put on a happy face.

© 2019 Jeanne Powell

She Kept Calling Time

Millicent kept calling time
everyone did, do you recall?
wrist watches were expensive
town clocks fell into disrepair.
When you needed to know,
really had to have the time
in the palm of your hands,
you simply called; it was that easy.
"At the tone the time will be…."
Her voice never changed.

The voice of time spoke with warmth and authority,
as though she knew that every single moment
her callers needed that calm reassurance.
"At the tone" and Millicent relaxed;
"the time will be" and Millicent listened;
"11:37 a.m." and Millicent smiled.
No electronic intrusions, no toll charge,
no disruptive mischief. Instead there was
goodness, tranquility, reassurance.

Until that dreadful, awful day
when time – just – stopped.
A voice from Corporate Central
announced the change in metallic tones.
She tried dialing the well-known number,
but there was no comfort to be found.
She could not reach the regal lady
who guarded the hours for so long.
 Millicent kept calling time, until
it was not possible anymore.

© 2019 Jeanne Powell

Nanking Where I Fell In Love
[Keh-Ming's favorite city]

Nanking where I fell in love.
did that really happen to me,
or a colorful daydream over oolong tea?
I have a passion for cities with a port,
imagine great voyages on historic days.
did I reside there in a previous life?
How thick were the leaves on my doorstep?

the first Chinese city to capture my heart
Nanking's lovely syllables haunt me still.
did I sail on a sampan or two or three?
Nanking near the Yangtse River on its way
to the East China Sea.
Why do I love this city of my dreams?
Rising phoenix-like from great pain
to rival Shanghai or Beijing?
in the glorious light rays of my dreams.

© 2019 Jeanne Powell

Westward Ho

Every evening he counted
the corners of his day,
the frost-bitten edges
where reason and hope collided
with regret and despair.
As he patrolled the four angles
of his daylight hours, he
was careful to follow
no guidelines but his own.
North was cold but wise,
South felt warm but unforgiving,
East projected a new day always
West promised the risk of escape.

© 2019 Jeanne Powell

The Hardest Job

5:00 a.m., and he is awake, ready to begin
the hardest job he ever held. Be the
night burglar even in the middle of the day.
Dress to blend with brick walls and cement
sidewalks. Throw in slices of neutral color
to glide past wooden fences and over
cobblestones. Carry gloves that don't offend
and a knapsack just large enough to evoke
suffering from the era of Charles Dickens.

Spy the bus transfer dropped on pavement,
scoop up the half lunch left on a park bench,
check out the bag of clothes abandoned beside
a street dumpster. Visiting Matilda
in the senior center? Pick a few flowers
in the park to take to her. Be sure no one
is looking. Music in Union Square? OK to
claim a seat, listen with joy and be free
from worry for a few minutes.

That reception at the antique store on Van Ness --
that was a good day. He walked right in with
regular guests, blending in the way he had.
He copped a five-pound block of good cheddar.
In his earnestness to complete the meal,
he asked out loud, "where is the bread?"
That was when he ceased to blend and so
was escorted out, five pounds of good cheddar
firmly under his arm. The sun was shining.
A good day, really.

© 2019 Jeanne Powell

She Doesn't Get Involved

Foraging at twilight,
her favorite moments
just enough light to retract, retrench,
circumnavigate, batten down,
navigate just north of the 13th month.
She gathers, commandeers,
begs and barters,
never using words, leery of compromise
for the things she has to have.
pantomime, sign language, warning shots
across the bow, ransom notes.
just enough light to leave a trace,
send apologies, kill the sentries.
taking only what she needs, a partridge,
a pear tree, a steak and kidney pie.
leaving a golden leaf or silver coin
no time for explanations
avoiding pity and regrets.
life in the fading moment in just enough light,
her getaway is clean.
she doesn't get involved.

© 2019 Jeanne Powell

Emergency

Hello, 9-1-1.
Yes, Hello. You need to send a patrol car to Hallidie Plaza.
What is the problem?
This guy is feeding the pigeons.
What is wrong, Ma'am?
Good grief! Are you deaf?
How may I help you?
You obviously don't live in this city.
Ma'am?
The city ordinance clearly says "do not feed the pigeons." It's posted on the kiosk at Cyril Magnin Alley.
Who is Cyril Magnin? Is he feeding the pigeons?
Were you raised in a barn? This guy is breaking the law. You need to send someone now to arrest him.
What is the problem, Ma'am?
Listen closely, you twit. This guy is potbellied, middle-aged, blond and sunburned. He is riding a green bicycle with a wire basket on the back and he is distributing birdseed from a burlap bag. He is wearing a purple shirt and gray Bermuda shorts with yellow sneakers. You can't miss him. The sign says don't feed the pigeons; this guy is a perpetrator.
Can you describe him, Ma'am?
Listen, you subcutaneous protohuman! Pull the wax out of your ears and sober up long enough to understand plain speaking! I'm leaving now. Otherwise I would have to reach through the telephone and strangle you!

Safe Surrender Site

Safe is not always as safe says it is.
possibilities always fear filled,
overrated, this safety business.
you can die in a millisecond
flash floods, sudden earth moves,
killer pigeons, a broken life line.
and what of it? Death needs to work
Death makes it safe to be alive.

Now about surrendering, that fearful
defeat or victory, it all depends on
who or what, where or why, even when.
such a business this endless bickering
over bad timing, guilt, punishment,
salvation. Isn't it just about relief,
no more journeying to endless sites
of compromise, rendering of injustice?

Pick a site, but not just any. Cite the
angels who guide you as justification
for searching for some safely woven
basket or warming blanket to lay down
your burden, hand off your shock & awe,
give birth to sense of new ground broken,
and know that the bell you ring at dawn
finally brings salvation to surrender.

Under California law unwanted infants can be surrendered to those fire stations and other emergerncy sites marked with the symbol of a blue baby.

© 2019 Jeanne Powell

Thoughts Upon Awakening

For no reason I awoke, eyes open and ears alert.
There was no sound to disturb my slumber.
Tenants upstairs were not moving furniture,
an activity which seemed to fascinate them.
Too early for Recology to bang garbage bins
in the courtyard. Yolanda and Marcello
had been evicted, so they no longer screamed
at each other in two languages at all hours.

Running through my mind was the refrain
from a popular song, a theme for a tv series:
"what if God were one of us?"
Why this lyric in my consciousness at 3 a.m.?

Suddenly I thought of Thursday mornings when
I have to set my internal clock to awaken at an
ungodly hour and take two buses, so that I could
arrive at Gabriella's writing seminar on time.

Last week as I walked in the fog past the office
of an architect, I spotted a small delivery box.
In a hurry, anxious to find a newspaper to read
before boarding the bus, I walked past the box.
I hesitated and turned around. The box was
setting on steps in front of the office, discarded.
Once it had held a small pizza, sufficient for one.

What caught my attention was a message printed
on the box in careful black lettering. It jumped out
at me through the early morning fog, through
the quiet exhaustion in my brain:

© 2019 Jeanne Powell

You have to remember your dreams to follow them.

You have to
remember your dreams
to follow them.

You have to remember your dreams to follow them.

Quickly I wrote the words, framed in haiku images, then I was able to drift back to sleep.

"What if God were one of us?"

© 2019 Jeanne Powell

About The Author

Jeanne Powell has earned degrees from WSU in Detroit and USF in San Francisco. She writes prose poems, flash fiction and short stage plays. Her previous books are MY OWN SILENCE and WORD DANCING, both published in second editions by Taurean Horn Press in 2013/2014. Jeanne's collection of essays, CAROUSEL, was published by Regent Press. For ten years Jeanne hosted an acclaimed spoken word series, "Celebration of the Word." She is the inspiration behind Meridien PressWorks™ which has published 20 authors since 1996. She has been an instructor in the CS, OLLI and UB programs on California campuses.

FEBRUARY VOICES

She writes...with the honesty of a survivor and the elegance of a stylist. Whether satirizing...or keening...or offering her own story with irony and gracefulness, her *Voices* are promising poems. I recommend that readers read them, and recommend that she write more.

— **Christopher Bernard**
Editor, *Caveat Lector*

CADENCES

Cadences is an impressive collection that fulfills the promise of *February Voices,* drawing us into its rhythms and meanings on many levels. These poems...sing and rage in ways that are compelling, enchanting and unforgettable.
— Dr. Louise M. Jefferson
Wayne State University

MY OWN SILENCE

My Own Silence is a testament against the worst type of silence--that of indifference. These are poems of conscience in which the poet ends her silence by transforming her outrage into unforgettable images.... Yet, despite the world's cruelty and sorrows, the poet finds much in which she can rejoice.... This is a book that looks hard at life...and embraces it in all its complexity.

— Dr. **Lucille Lang Day**
author of *Wild One* and *Infinities*

My Own Silence is a vibrant, cohesive collection of story-poems, with bold beginnings and endings neatly tucked. The writer spins dramatic filaments into poetic gold with a rhythmic ear and a robust voice. Cousin to Whitman, Jordan, Collins -- Jeanne Powell's literary threads are expertly woven into America's tapestry of struggle and redemption.

— **Stephen Kopel**
author of *Spritz* and *Tender Absurdities*

CAROUSEL

At a time when the confessional mode has banished American poetry to one vast self-mirroring island, the work of Jeanne Powell nudges us again and again to break out of our little selves. Whether celebrating the triumphs of Australia's champion Aboriginal athlete Cathy Freeman, berating a hellish vacation in the Sierra foothills, disclosing the subtle and not so subtle pain of social injustice, or commemorating a powerful, dancing mother reared in the big band swing era, Powell rocks. Unfailingly, the open-hearted spirit of her prose and poetry allows us to re-experience our membership in one another.

— **Al Young**
California Poet Laureate Emeritus

www.ingramcontent.com/pod-product-compliance
Lightning Source LLC
Chambersburg PA
CBHW020703300426
44112CB00007B/495